Thomas Paine

VIP
Very Interesting People

Bite-sized biographies of Britain's most fascinating historical figures

1. **William Shakespeare**	*Peter Holland*
2. **George Eliot**	*Rosemary Ashton*
3. **Charles Dickens**	*Michael Slater*
4. **Charles Darwin**	*Adrian Desmond, James Moore, and Janet Browne*
5. **Isaac Newton**	*Richard S. Westfall*
6. **Elizabeth I**	*Patrick Collinson*
7. **George III**	*John Cannon*
8. **Benjamin Disraeli**	*Jonathan Parry*
9. **Christopher Wren**	*Kerry Downes*
10. **John Ruskin**	*Robert Hewison*
11. **James Joyce**	*Bruce Stewart*
12. **John Milton**	*Gordon Campbell*
13. **Jane Austen**	*Marilyn Butler*
14. **Henry VIII**	*Eric Ives*
15. **Queen Victoria**	*K. D. Reynolds and H. C. G. Matthew*
16. **Winston Churchill**	*Paul Addison*
17. **Oliver Cromwell**	*John Morrill*
18. **Thomas Paine**	*Mark Philp*
19. **J. M. W. Turner**	*Luke Herrmann*
20. **William and Mary**	*Tony Claydon and W. A. Speck*

Thomas Paine

VIP
Very Interesting People

Mark Philp

OXFORD
UNIVERSITY PRESS

OXFORD
UNIVERSITY PRESS

Great Clarendon Street, Oxford OX2 6DP

Oxford University Press is a department of the University of Oxford.
It furthers the University's objective of excellence in research, scholarship,
and education by publishing worldwide in

Oxford New York

Auckland Cape Town Dar es Salaam Hong Kong Karachi
Kuala Lumpur Madrid Melbourne Mexico City Nairobi
New Delhi Shanghai Taipei Toronto

With offices in

Argentina Austria Brazil Chile Czech Republic France Greece
Guatemala Hungary Italy Japan Poland Portugal Singapore
South Korea Switzerland Thailand Turkey Ukraine Vietnam

Oxford is a registered trade mark of Oxford University Press
in the UK and in certain other countries

Published in the United States
by Oxford University Press Inc., New York

First published in the *Oxford Dictionary of National Biography* 2004
This paperback edition first published 2007

First published 2007

British Library Cataloguing in Publication Data

Data available

Library of Congress Cataloging in Publication Data

Data available

Typeset by SPI Publisher Services, Pondicherry, India
Printed in Great Britain
on acid-free paper by
Clays Ltd, St Ives plc

ISBN 978-0-19-953458-6

1

Contents

Preface

Some writers resist posthumous consensus. Thomas Paine is a case in point. Biographers in the early nineteenth century were driven by strongly partisan sentiments—some for him, some vehemently against—and even more recent studies of Paine have an edge of partiality and commitment. To give some idea of the range: the former American President John Adams (1735–1826), writing at the end of his long life, reflected in the following terms on the impact of Paine:

> I am willing you should call this the Age of Frivolity as you do, and would not object if you had named it the Age of Folly, Vice, Frenzy, Brutality, Daemons, Buonaparte, Tom Paine, or

> the Age of the Burning Brand from the Bottomless Pit, or anything but the Age of Reason. I know not whether any man in the world has had more influence on its inhabitants or affairs for the last thirty years than Tom Paine. There can be no severer Satyr on the age. For such a mongrel between pig and puppy, begotten by a wild boar on a bitch wolf, never before in any age of the world was suffered the poltroonery of mankind, to run such a career of mischief. Call it then the Age of Paine. (D. F. Hawke, *Paine*, 1974, 7)

While the most recent book on Paine by Christopher Hitchens concludes: 'In a time when both rights and reason are under several kinds of open and covert attack, the life and writings of Thomas Paine will always be part of the arsenal on which we shall need to depend' (C. Hitchens, *Thomas Paine's Rights of Man*, 2006, 142).

This partisanship over Paine has not always served the interest of scholarship and there are many areas of his life, activities, and interests that deserve more attention. His involvement in France and its politics has not been examined in much detail since the early work of A. O. Aldridge in the 1950s; there has been relatively little work undertaken on Paine's scientific and engineering interests; and while Paine's historical reputation has been battled over, his ideas have not, for the most part, featured in contemporary political theory.

That there is more to be done was brought home to me rather forcibly when, having bought my younger daughter Hannah a copy of Martin Kemp's recent book on Leonardo, I found in it a sketch of proportions of a tree that Paine essentially copied in a letter to Jefferson in 1788 to demonstrate how to assess the amount of wood in a tree. This tiny shaft of light on one of Paine's influences contrasts sharply with our considerable ignorance about Paine's sources—abetted by his own denial that he had ever read such seminal works in political theory as John Locke's *Two Treatises*. Recent work has, however, noted the important connections between Paine and

Adam Smith, and attention has also been paid by Gareth Stedman Jones (*An End to Poverty*, 2004) to the involvement of Paine with members of the *Comité de Mendicité de la Constituante* and to the impact this undoubtedly had on his welfare proposals at the end of the second part of *Rights of Man*. Moreover, contemporary political philosophers and economists are now showing renewed interest in some of Paine's proposals in *Rights of Man* and *Agrarian Justice* for a basic income for all those coming of age, and his account of the nature of representative democracy has also been the subject of scrutiny as scholars try to understand quite why modern democracy feels so disappointing!

Nonetheless, there remains much to be done to come fully to grips with the intermingling of influences, and Paine's own impact, on his various domains of activity—America, England and France; experimentation and engineering; politics and religion. It is a testament to his importance that as we become better informed about his life and his influences, so too will we become better informed about his times. But this means that this 'life', originally written for the *Oxford Dictionary of National Biography*, is not the final word on Paine and his importance; like our understanding of him it is, at best, a report on work in progress.

Mark Philp

January 2007

About the author

Mark Philp is a Fellow and Tutor in Politics at Oriel College, Oxford, and a former Head of the University's Politics and International Relations Department. He has written widely on aspects of late eighteenth-century political thought and social history with books on Thomas Paine and William Godwin and editions of both. His recent work includes *Napoleon and the Invasion of Britain* (with Alexandra Franklin, 2003), *Resisting Napoleon: The British Response to the Threat of Invasion, 1797–1815* (2006), and *Political Conduct* (2007).

1 Path to the New World

Thomas Paine (1737–1809), author and revolutionary, was born in Thetford, Norfolk, on 29 January 1737, the first of two children of Joseph Pain (1708–1787), stay-maker and tenant farmer, and Frances Cocke (1697–*c.*1790), daughter of Thomas Cocke, attorney and town clerk of Thetford. Paine's only sibling, Elizabeth, born a year later, died aged seven months. Paine's father was a Quaker and his mother an Anglican, and it is likely that Paine was baptized into the Anglican church, as was his sister.

Stay-maker and exciseman

Paine's father retained his Quaker principles and, though Thomas was confirmed, his father forbade him to learn Latin when he attended the local grammar school at the age of seven. He received a basic education, in which he showed some signs of mathematical ability and a bent for poetry; a short poem to a crow, supposedly written when Paine was eight, shows a certain prescience: 'Here lies the body of John Crow / Who once was high but now is low / Ye brother crows take warning all / For as you rise, so must you fall'. When he was twelve his father removed him from school and took him on as an apprentice.

In *Rights of Man*, Paine recounts how, as a youth of little more than sixteen, influenced by the maritime stories of the Revd William Knowles, a master of Thetford grammar school, he enlisted on the *Terrible*, a privateer commanded by Captain Death (fitted out at execution dock and carrying on board Lieutenant Devil and Mr Ghost, the ship's surgeon). It is likely he was nearer twenty, but he was fortunate in yielding to his father's pleas to stay ashore, since the ship lost all but 26 of her crew of 200 in an engagement. Within six months he enlisted again, this time on the *King of Prussia*, also a privateer, but one which enjoyed considerably greater success. The exact movements of Paine at this time are uncertain. Either between his privateering bouts, or subsequently, he worked in London for John Morris, a stay-maker on Hanover Street, Long Acre, in Covent Garden. Some biographers suggest that Paine's later account in *The Age of Reason*—that he attended the scientific lectures of Benjamin Martin and James Ferguson—refers to this period, but he may equally be referring to other times spent in London, especially 1766–8, which fit more exactly with the little evidence available and with his memory. In the spring of 1758 he worked for the stay-maker Benjamin Grace in Dover, and the following year established his own business in Sandwich, where he is reputed to have taken up as an occasional Methodist preacher. On 27 September 1759 he married Mary Lambert (*d.* 1760), who died in childbirth the following year after the couple moved to Margate following business difficulties.

After his wife's death Paine resolved to abandon the stay-making business and sought a career in the excise, the occupation of his wife's father. He returned home to live with his parents while he learned the skills of the trade at the hands of Henry Cocksedge, recorder of Thetford. He was accepted into the service and received a first appointment to Grantham in December 1762, moving subsequently to Alford, also in Lincolnshire, in August 1764. His career was cut short in August 1765 when he was dismissed from his post for 'stamping'—certifying examinations not actually made. He was forced to resume staymaking, finding work at Diss under a Mr Gudgeon, from where he wrote apologizing to the excise board. He was reinstated on 4 July 1766 but had to await a new posting. In the interim he taught first at a school run by Daniel Noble in Mill Yard, Leman Street, Goodman's Field, London, and then from January 1767 in a school in Kensington run by a Mr Gardiner. His teaching seems to have kept him adequately provided for, since he was able to turn down an excise post in Grampound, Cornwall, in May 1767 in the hope of finding something closer to London. This is the longest period Paine spent in the capital, and it may have been at this time that he developed his scientific interests. On 19 February 1768 he accepted the post of excise officer in Lewes, where he took up lodgings with Samuel Ollive, an innkeeper, and his family, eventually sharing with them in the setting up of a tobacco mill to supplement his income.

Paine settled comfortably in Lewes. His name appears alongside Ollive's in records of the town's governing body and he was a vocal member of the local debating club, known as the Headstrong Club, where he developed a reputation as an obstinate haranguer. He was also known as a player of bowls and as a skater, with his skills earning him the nickname the Commodore. His friend from this period, the bookseller and reformer Thomas 'Clio' Rickman, described him as about 5 feet 10 inches, rather athletic, and broad-shouldered. His eye 'was full, brilliant and singularly piercing', and had in it the 'muse of fire'. He was cleanly dressed, 'wore his hair cued with side curls and powdered and looked altogether like a gentleman of the old French school' (Rickman, xv). In manners he was easy and gracious, his knowledge was universal and boundless, and while in private company he was fascinating, in mixed company he was reticent and was no public speaker. Paine's political views were whig: he was 'tenacious of his opinions which were bold, acute, and independent, and which he maintained with ardour, elegance, and argument' (ibid., 38). Although he subsequently claimed that America had made him an author, biographers agree that he wrote several poems, a mock drama, *The Trial of Farmer Carter's Dog Porter*, and some prose pieces, several of which he published a few years later in America. In one of the most stable periods of his life he lived for 'several years in habits of intimacy with a very respectable, sensible, and convivial set of acquaintance, who were entertained with his witty sallies and informed by his more serious conversations' (ibid.).

Leaving England

Samuel Ollive died in July 1769, leaving his widow, Esther, and daughter, Elizabeth, in poor circumstances. For propriety's sake, Paine took up lodgings elsewhere, but the following year he joined the Ollives in opening a shop, and on 26 March 1771 he married Elizabeth (*c*.1749–1808) who was at least ten years his junior. The following year he was nominated to press the excisemen's case for improved pay and conditions in London. He wrote his first political pamphlet, *The Case of the Officers of Excise*, and late in 1772 travelled to London. He corresponded with Oliver Goldsmith and developed (or expanded) his acquaintance with members of scientific circles, including the mathematician and excise commissioner, George Lewis Scott. It is also possible that his acquaintance with the Philadelphia politician and natural philosopher, Benjamin Franklin, dates from this visit. In the cause of the excisemen he was unsuccessful. He failed to have the matter brought before parliament, and the petition he carried with the signatures of some 3000 excisemen was ignored. He returned to Lewes in mid-April 1773 to face the collapse of his business affairs.

Little or nothing is known of Paine in the year subsequent to his return, but the following April he received a double blow, being dismissed from the excise on 8 April 1774 for 'having quitted his business, without obtaining the Board's Leave for so doing, and being gone off on account of the Debts which he hath contracted', and being forced to sell off by auction on 14 April 'all the household furniture, stock in trade and other effects... also a horse tobacco and snuff mill, with all the utensils for cutting tobacco and grinding off snuff' (Conway, *Life*, 1.29–30). Moreover, in May 1774 Paine and his wife separated, with a formal document being signed on 4 June 1774. Twenty years later the separation generated extensive prurient speculation, with reports that the marriage was not consummated, but Paine remained characteristically reticent: 'It is nobody's business but my own: I had cause for it, but I will name it to no one' (Rickman, 47). The settlement gave Elizabeth her full inheritance from her father and left her free to trade.

The April sale must have left Paine with some money, since we have no record of him working between April and October, when, carrying a letter of introduction from Benjamin Franklin, he paid for a berth on a ship to America. Early biographies of Paine, especially the deeply hostile lives by Francis Oldys (the pseudonym of George Chalmers) and James Cheetham, were often maliciously inventive in their reconstruction of Paine's first thirty-seven years, ascribing his first wife's death to his cruelty and accusing him of a variety of fraudulent practices. Despite his friendship with Paine, Rickman is no more informed about the early years. Subsequent biographers devoting space to this period of Paine's life have compensated for the paucity of evidence by literary licence and speculation. What is clear is that Paine's early life was not a success and that he was probably heartily glad to leave England behind him and to embark on a fresh set of challenges in the new world.

When his ship docked in Philadelphia on 30 November 1774 Paine had to be carried off on a stretcher. He was so weakened by acute seasickness and putrid fever that it took him several weeks to recover. Franklin's letter introduced

Paine to his son-in-law, Richard Bache, who sought pupils for him to teach, and he also became acquainted with Robert Aitkin, in whose Front Street bookshop he frequently browsed. Aitkin offered to employ him as the editor of a new journal he was planning, the *Pennsylvania Magazine*, for an annual salary of £50. Aitkin proposed to leave the detailed editorial work to Paine while retaining the right to control the policy and content of the magazine. Paine's contributions have been much disputed as none appears under his name and various pen names were used, but he wrote between seventeen and twenty-six pieces for it over the following eighteen months, including an essay against slavery which brought him an introduction to the physician Benjamin Rush, and pieces on the deaths of the army officers James Wolfe and Robert Clive which raised issues of British colonial policy that were highly pertinent given the growing tensions between Britain and her American colonies.

Paine's developing literary reputation introduced him into political circles in Philadelphia, through which he became acquainted with the issues of the day and many of the leading activists. As he later commented, he 'thought it very hard to have the country set on fire about my ears almost the moment I got into it' (Conway, *Life*, 1.55–6). After growing tension between Britain and the Americans, active conflict broke out in April 1775 with skirmishes between British troops and American militiamen at Lexington and Concord. A second continental congress was called in May, at which further moves towards reconciliation with Britain were made. However, these too failed, and by December the colonies were openly denying parliament's right to rule them directly, while continuing to look to George III as their protector and king.

Common Sense: 'the cause of all mankind'

In the autumn of 1775, encouraged by Rush, Paine began work on a pamphlet putting the case for independence. Although he read aloud drafts to Rush and showed a completed draft to the astronomer David Rittenhouse, Benjamin

Franklin, and the Massachusetts politician Samuel Adams, the work was wholly Paine's—except for the title, for which Rush claimed credit. The result, *Common Sense*, 'written by an Englishman', was the most widely distributed pamphlet of the American War of Independence, and has the strongest claim to have made independence seem both desirable and attainable to the wavering colonists. Paine's ability to write in accessible prose, and to convey his beliefs as simply the promptings of common sense, was coupled with his insistence that the issues between Britain and America were of universal import. This was not a little local difficulty. Rather,

> the cause of America is in a great measure the cause of all mankind . . . 'Tis not the concern of a day, a year, or an age; posterity are virtually involved in the contest, and will be more or less affected, even to the end of time, by the proceedings now. (*Complete Writings*, 1.3, 17)

It is a universal cause because America remains the providentially chosen asylum for liberty while Europe crumbles into despotism.

Society, Paine announces in the opening paragraphs of the pamphlet, 'in every state is a blessing, but government even in its best state is but a necessary evil; in its worst state [it is] an intolerable one' (ibid., 1.4). People are driven into society by the multiple benefits it brings; government only becomes necessary as vice develops, and it best serves the end of protecting freedom and security by taking a representative and republican form. The much vaunted constitution of England is an amalgam of pure republican elements with the remains of monarchical and aristocratic tyrannies, which are wholly incompatible with the preservation of freedom. Government by kings runs contrary to the natural equality of man, ''Tis a form of government which the word of God bears testimony against, and blood will attend it' (ibid., 1.16). This is what has happened in America: following the commencement of hostilities in April, all plans for reconciliation must be jettisoned and Americans must recognize that they are dealing not with a 'mother country' but with a tyrannical oppressor. Moreover, America cannot reap a single advantage from reconciliation that could not be had from independence, while 'the injuries and disadvantages we sustain by that connection, are without number' (ibid., 1.20). 'Reconciliation is *now* a fallacious dream', since, citing John Milton: 'never can true reconcilement grow where wounds of deadly hate have pierced so deep' (ibid., 1.23). Having shown that the obvious and necessary step is independence, Paine sketches a plan of self-government for the country, which is to begin from a continental conference to frame a continental charter and a government 'securing freedom and property to all men, and above all the free exercise of religion'. In contrast to Europe, 'in America THE LAW IS KING' (ibid., 1.29).

The pamphlet appeared on the same day as news of George III's intransigent response to the colonists' petitions arrived in Philadelphia. It was able to turn widespread dismay at the king's failure into a recognition that monarchical government was simply not to be trusted. The success of the pamphlet was unparalleled. Rival second editions appeared within a matter of three weeks, and Paine turned against his publisher,

Robert Bell, whom he accused of pirating a second edition. Seven editions appeared in Philadelphia alone, with other cities also producing editions from the beginning of February. Despite this, Paine made no money by the pamphlet, and probably financed an edition from his own resources to promote circulation. His objective was to ensure that the argument for independence should be spread throughout America. By April 1776 he was claiming that 120,000 copies had been sold, and he later gave a figure of 150,000 for America alone. It is unlikely that he greatly exaggerated. As Benjamin Rush recalled in July 1776: 'Its effects were sudden and extensive upon the American mind. It was read by public men, repeated in clubs, spouted in Schools, and in one instance, delivered from the pulpit instead of a sermon by a clergyman in Connecticut' (*Autobiography of Benjamin Rush*, 114–15).

The pamphlet also produced a flood of criticism, beginning with James Chalmers's *Plain Truth*. Some critics resisted independence while others, such as John Adams's highly influential

Thoughts on Government, offered more nuanced and subtle criticism of Paine's enthusiasm for simple, democratically elected and centralized government. Overnight Paine became a controversialist, embarking on a series of essays (signed The Forester), engaging with some of the criticisms raised against his arguments for independence, and becoming embroiled in both local Philadelphia politics and those around the continental congress based there. On 2 July congress declared independence, and on 4 July it approved Thomas Jefferson's declaration (in which some have thought Paine had a hand).

American patriot

2

War of Independence

A few days later Paine joined a body of Pennsylvania volunteers who marched towards New York. The anticipated British attack never materialized, and Paine spent the summer as secretary to Daniel Roberdeau, the commander of the flying camp. When it was disbanded he travelled to Fort Lee and served as aide-de-camp to General Nathanael Greene, who became a close friend. He also served as a field correspondent, puffing American successes in small skirmishes and supporting the decisions of Greene and George Washington despite their frequent military blunders. The retreat of Washington's army towards Trenton and Philadelphia at the end of 1776 produced despondency in those who six months before had been enthusiastic for independence.

When Paine visited Philadelphia he found the people in a 'deplorable and melancholy condition... afraid to speak and almost to think, the public presses stopped, and nothing in circulation but fears and falsehoods' (*Complete Writings*, 2.1164). To rouse their spirits he produced *The American Crisis*, the first of thirteen letters designed to muster the American people to the cause and to set straight the record of military affairs. It is a resounding piece of political rhetoric, with as powerful an opening as any political pamphlet published:

> These are the times that try men's souls. The summer soldier and the sun-shine patriot will, in this crisis, shrink from the service of his country: but he that stands it *now*, deserves the thanks of man and woman. Tyranny, like hell, is not easily conquered: yet we have this consolation with us, that the harder the conflict, the more glorious the triumph. What we obtain too

cheap, we esteem too lightly; it is dearness only that gives everything its value. (ibid., 1.50)

Tradition has it that Washington ordered the pamphlet to be read aloud to the troops on the evening of Christmas day before the battle of Trenton.

With the American War of Independence Paine had found a cause and an apposite voice with which to advocate it. In reinventing himself as an American patriot, he discovered a gift for articulating the hopes and fears of ordinary men and women in ways which revealed to them their higher purpose as Americans. John Quincy Adams later described Paine as having 'no country, no affections that constitute the pillars of patriotism' (Hawke, 33). Some of Paine's comments encourage such a view—in his *Crisis No. 7* he insisted 'my principle is universal. My attachment is to all the world, and not to any particular part' (*Complete Writings*, 2.146), and his concern for America was a concern for the principles it represented—liberty, security, and republican government (which he understood as representative democracy and the sovereignty of the people). He never wavered in his commitment to these principles, but nor did he ever doubt that America offered the greatest hope for their realization. His writings during the War of Independence, including *The American Crisis* and subsequent *Crisis* essays, were often directed at particular events and matters of local importance, but he rarely failed to lift the issue onto the larger stage of the cause of freedom against the despotism of Britain and its corrupt monarchy.

Paine also became still more practically involved in the struggle, coupling his need to make some money with his commitment to the cause by accepting a job as secretary to a congressional commission to treat with Native American peoples on the Susquhanna. In March 1777, when congress returned to Philadelphia, he was appointed secretary of a new committee for foreign affairs. This relatively undemanding post left him time to work on a projected history of the American War of Independence for which he was collecting materials. Late in the summer, when the British landed in Delaware Bay and marched towards Philadelphia, defeating the Americans at Brandywine Creek on 11 September, Paine was forced to pack his papers and quit the city. After a brief stay with his friend Colonel Joseph Kirkbride in Bordentown, New Jersey, he set off to find Washington's army, arriving during the battle of Germantown. He stayed only a few days, but returned in October after Timothy Matlack, secretary of Pennsylvania's executive council, suggested he act as an observer to ensure a more constant intelligence of Washington's army. Over the next six months Paine divided his time between visits to Valley Forge, where the army waited out the winter, the hospitality of Kirkbride's house, and, after January 1778, William Henry's home in Lancaster, where his reported indolence caused considerable resentment among those more active in the cause.

In the spring of 1778, following British proposals for peace and the prospect of a political treaty with France, Paine's optimism grew. With French support, he believed, the Americans could bring the war to a close. Although the British proposals were rejected they vacated Philadelphia, and in June congress returned to take up its business there. Paine's energies also revived: *The American Crisis*, number 6, in October 1778, attacked the British peace proposals, and was followed in November by number 7, explaining why the British would never conquer the Americans and inciting the British people to overthrow their government. In December he also wrote a series of letters defending the unicameral form of the Pennsylvanian constitution, something which he had first commented on over a year previously in his *Candid and Critical Remarks on a Letter signed Ludlow* (1777).

Foreign affairs and military finance

Paine's responsibilities as secretary had not been onerous, and it may well have been intended as a sinecure, but he was encouraged by friends to see it in a larger light, leading his detractors to accuse him of styling himself 'secretary of foreign affairs'. His sense of the importance of his office led to the first major set-back in his American career. Silas Deane was one of three commissioners (with Franklin and Arthur Lee) with responsibility for securing financial support under cover of a commercial treaty with France. The covert nature of the gift of arms and supplies enabled Caron de Beaumarchais, who headed the company which acted as a front for the arrangement, to demand payment from congress. When Deane wrote from Paris supporting Beaumarchais's claim against congress for 4.5 million livres he was ordered home to report. On his arrival in Philadelphia in the summer of 1778 opinion rapidly polarized between those who accepted his claim to have been a loyal servant of American interests and those who saw him as profiteering. With his knowledge of the secret arrangements with France, Paine felt obliged to attack Deane, but his veiled accusations were perplexing for observers and infuriated Deane's supporters, who physically assaulted Paine on the street on two occasions. None the less, he maintained a stream of letters attacking both

 Deane and mercantile interests in congress for profiteering.

Broadening his attack increased Paine's enemies and blunted the force of his main argument. Moreover, in claiming that the supplies from France were a gift, Paine betrayed a secret which was extremely embarrassing to France. The French minister, Conrad Gérard, flatly denied the gift and demanded that congress repudiate Paine's allegations. When congress complied Paine offered his resignation, but refused to apologize. After several days of intense debate congress, by the narrowest margin, accepted his resignation, sparing him the indignity of dismissal. Gérard, rather surprisingly, then offered Paine a large sum (Paine claimed it was in excess of £700) to write supporting French interests and the alliance with America. Paine refused, but seemed mollified until he discovered that Gérard had thanked congress for their repudiation of Paine's 'false and dangerous insinuations' (Hawke, 92). He sought a retraction from Gérard and, on failing, secluded himself in his rooms, shunning all company and writing eight further pieces to vindicate his conduct in the affair and establish Deane's culpability. The affair gradually subsided, but it was not until two years later, when Deane wrote a series of letters encouraging American union with Britain, that his supporters finally questioned Deane's integrity.

Paine's seclusion ended when financial difficulties led him to accept a job as clerk in Owen Brindle's merchant office. He also accepted appointment to two committees to scrutinize the business affairs of the financier and politician, Robert Morris. He returned to print in the summer of 1779 with a series of letters defending America's Newfoundland fishing rights. The rights were a source of contention in negotiations with Britain, and Gérard and others believed that insisting on them would only prolong the war. During the controversy Whitehead Humphreys, a local merchant, penned a series of vicious attacks on Paine until he was lectured firmly on the freedoms and duties of the press by Paine's supporters. In November he was fully rehabilitated when he was appointed as clerk to the Pennsylvania assembly, and in the following year he was awarded an honorary MA from the University of Pennsylvania.

Paine was convinced that a principal obstacle to American success was inadequate federal finance. A few days before the dramatic surrender of General Lincoln and some 5000 American troops at Charleston in May 1780, he drew out the salary he was owed as clerk and sent half of the sum, $500, to Blair M'Clenaghan as a priming contribution for a voluntary subscription fund to support the recruiting system. As a result a permanent securities subscription was established, which developed into the Bank of North America and supplied the army throughout the rest of the war. The bank, and the subscription initiative, exemplify Paine's conviction that the interests of the poorer and wealthier classes were essentially identical and that each could be prevailed upon to contribute their due to the war effort.

The same conviction informed his *Crisis Extraordinary* in October 1780, in which he argued for the acceptance of higher rates of taxation to support the war. The land claims of Virginia to the western territories also drew him into controversy, partly because Maryland (a small state with no adjacent territories) refused to ratify the articles of confederation without limitations being placed on territorial claims, thereby leaving America without a constitution, and partly because it opened the possibility of raising federal income. Drawing heavily on information supplied by the Indiana Company, Paine's *Public Good* (1780) argued that the western territories should be recognized as the property of the federal government, and might accordingly be sold to support the war effort. The pamphlet turned many Virginians against Paine, and his acceptance of shares and cash from the Indiana Company led to allegations of his being a company hireling.

Paine also sought more practical involvement in the conflict. He asked congress to support him on a secret mission to England to write encouraging efforts for peace and recognition of American independence, thereby following up suggestions in *Crisis No. 8* that the conflict be somehow brought onto British soil. Late in the day he was dissuaded by friends who feared that, if caught, the British would use him as a reprisal for the American execution of the spy Major André. However, he welcomed the suggestion of Colonel John Laurens, the son of Paine's friend Henry Laurens, the former president of congress, that he act as his secretary while special envoy to France. When objections were raised in congress to Paine acting in an official capacity, he agreed to go as Laurens's companion, paying his own expenses. They sailed in February 1781, with an eventful voyage encompassing icebergs and the liberation of a Venetian merchantman from a Scottish cutter.

In France Paine made a number of new acquaintances. Franklin's grandnephew, Jonathan Williams, found him 'a pleasant as well as sensible man' (Aldridge, *Man of Reason*, 87). Elkanah Wilson, on the other hand, described him as 'coarse and uncouth in his manners, loathsome in his appearance, and a disgusting egoist, rejoicing most in talking of himself and reading the effusions of his mind' (Hawke, 116). Moreover, Wilson claimed he was filthy of appearance, awkward and unseemly in address, and that he stank from being treated for scabies—a fault Wilson cured by insisting Paine took a bath. In Paris, Paine had little social life, being received only at Franklin's (then American ambassador) and at Laurens's hotel. Laurens's trip was successful (although credit for this seems best placed with Franklin) and they returned to America in August with substantial funding.

In search of an income

Paine himself returned penniless: he had no income and claimed to have spent all his savings. Because of his financial plight and his sense that he was unappreciated, he talked of quitting America for Europe, where he hoped to live by his pen. However, Robert Morris wrote to him in September 1781 encouraging him to write in support of taxation for funding the war, and over the next six months Paine and Morris reached an agreement whereby congress paid him $800 per annum to urge state legislatures to allow the federal government sufficient tax income and to press for the extension of federal powers (the first fruits of which were his *Six Letters to Rhode Island*, 1782–3). Paine needed the money, but he was advocating a cause to which he was already publicly committed. He also regarded the payment as part compensation from congress for the fact that he had neglected his own interests by publishing without thought of personal profit. On several occasions he pressed both Morris and Washington for official financial recognition of his services to the revolution. It also seems likely that he received some payment from the French ministry. Barbé de Marbois, the French chargé d'affaires, reported in April 1782 that Paine had published nothing since his return from France without previously consulting La Luzerne (Gérard's successor as French minister to America), and it is likely that *Crisis No. 11* was a result of French encouragement, repudiating as it did the possibility of America making a peace with Britain independently of her allies France and Spain.

Paine's projected history of the American Revolution never materialized. La Luzerne claimed he was too indolent for such a task and it is true that his forte lay elsewhere. However, the work he had done doubtless contributed to his decision to write a refutation of the Abbé Raynal's *A Philosophical ... History of the ... Indies*, the last volume of which was published in translation in 1781 and dealt with the American War of Independence. Paine objected to Raynal's claims that the war arose entirely from a dispute over taxation and that peace efforts had been hampered by the Americans' alliance with France. His *Letter to the Abbé Raynal, on the Affairs of North America* (1782) is an exemplary piece of diplomacy, carefully establishing the self-driven character of the American War of Independence and implicitly denying a special significance to France's involvement. It is also an immensely optimistic work, which insists that the American cause cannot be understood wholly in pragmatic terms, but is evidence of a progressive enlightenment which is bringing man from barbarism to civilization. Commerce is central to this process:

just as it once formed men into societies to furnish their wants and harmonize their interests, so too will it operate between nations, when guided by reason rather than the interests of despotic regimes, to end war through the emergence of universal society of mutual benefit. The *Letter* did much to secure Paine's European reputation; it also earned him both gratitude and financial reward from the French minister.

When the war finally ended Paine required a means of subsistence. On Robert Morris's advice, he drew up a letter to congress outlining his services and suggesting that if it were to make him financially independent he could undertake a history of the war. A committee was appointed to consider his suggestion and recommended he be appointed official historian, but congress took no action. In June 1784 the New York assembly presented him with a farm in New Rochelle confiscated from a tory, but similar initiatives in the Virginia assembly failed because of local opposition. Following further letters from Paine, congress agreed in October to pay him $3000 for his services, and the following March Pennsylvania set aside £500 as a temporary recompense for Paine, while referring to congress the matter of any further grant. Paine bought a farm in Bordentown, near his friend Colonel Kirkbride, having decided to rent out the New Rochelle property.

Hope of further support from Pennsylvania was ended by conflicts over the Bank of North America and the issue of paper currency in the aftermath of the war. The assembly sought to repeal the bank's charter following its opposition to issuing paper currency. Paine remained a staunch defender of the bank and its charter, and in February 1786 published *Dissertation on Government; the Affairs of the Bank; and Paper Money*, followed by a number of letters amplifying his position. Many of his contemporaries saw Paine's defence of the bank as a reactionary and élitist move, and assumed he had been paid to champion the interests of property against those of the people, but his position is consistent with his belief in the independence of financial institutions and the dangers of paper currency. In the course of his defence Paine insisted both that sovereignty could not bind successive generations (a key principle in his *Rights of Man*) and that contracts between the state and particular individuals (such as charters) could not subsequently be revised without the consent of both parties. On Paine's account the assembly was acting unconstitutionally in attempting to repeal the charter.

Attempts at bridge building

Once established at Bordentown, Paine's interests turned towards scientific experiments. He was invited by Washington to stay near Princeton, where they spent a day investigating marsh gas in a local creek, and he experimented on a smokeless candle with Franklin. His energies were increasingly absorbed, however, on his plans for a single-span bridge, constructed in sections from iron and designed to span large distances without the use of piers. Late in 1785 he hired John Hall, a carpenter and mechanic recently emigrated from England, to work with him on a model of the bridge which he hoped to persuade the Pennsylvania assembly to build across the Schuylkill river. He may well have drawn his ideas from models he had seen on his trip to France, where proposals for single-arched iron bridges had recently been discussed at the Royal Academy of Sciences.

Paine's design was distinctive in constructing the arch on the model of a spider's web, on the grounds that 'when Nature enabled this insect to make a web, she taught it the best means of putting it together' (Aldridge, *Man of Reason*, 109). Hall and Paine began with models made from wood, and in May 1786 set to work on a model in iron. In December he took a single-arched model of wrought iron to Franklin's house and demonstrated it first to Franklin and subsequently to the Pennsylvania assembly. The cost of building a bridge of iron was high, American foundries being small, and although the assembly discussed the project no action was taken. This discouraging response, combined with a long-standing sense on Paine's part that he was inadequately appreciated in his adopted land and had little role to play in the newly constituted republic, determined him to take his model to France to solicit expert opinion and find financial backing to build the bridge. He sought letters of introduction to members of the French court from Franklin and embarked for France in April 1787.

Paine landed in Le Havre in May 1787 and set off for Paris. His letters of introduction brought him into contact with French scientific circles, and he renewed his acquaintance with Thomas Jefferson (now American minister in Paris). He presented his model to the Academy of Sciences in July, which reported favourably at the end of August. Paine then left France to visit his parents, while Jefferson and the marquis de Lafayette continued to encourage the government to use his design for a bridge across the Seine. He returned to Paris briefly in December and, once back in England, sent Jefferson a proposal for financing the bridge in France, asking him to read it and, if appropriate, have it translated and communicated to the ministry.

The search for finance for the bridge continued until the summer of 1788, when Paine decided to concentrate on securing support in Britain. He applied for and received letters patent and engaged the Walker brothers' ironworks in Rotherham to construct an arch of 90 feet, this being a more practical proposition than his original aspiration for a 250 foot span (and one which could be accomplished indoors). He remained in Rotherham until November 1788, when the first half was completed, and then returned to London. In April 1789 the arch was assembled, to his great satisfaction. He entered an agreement with the Walkers that they should manufacture a complete bridge of 110 feet, to be erected over the Thames and then put up for sale, with proceeds being divided equally. The bridge was cast in Rotherham and shipped down to London, arriving in May 1790. It was assembled on a field halfway between Paddington and Marylebone near a public house, the Yorkshire Stingo, where Paine and his mechanic, a Mr Buel, took up residence. The bridge was completed in September 1790 and attracted public interest, along with

38 a fair amount of criticism—not least from the American diplomatist Gouverneur Morris, who found himself living uncomfortably close to Paine and noted that 'it is not so handsome as he [Paine] thinks it is. Qu. also whether it be as strong. It has a very light appearance however' (*Diary of the French Revolution*, 1.589). By October the wood abutments on which the bridge rested began to yield beneath the load and the metal began to rust in the poorer weather. The Walkers repossessed the ironwork and transported it back to Rotherham, and by the end of November Paine had become wholly engaged in political affairs.

3

An age of revolutions

Paine's *Rights of Man*

When he had arrived in France in 1787, Paine had formed a friendship with the secretary of the archbishop of Toulouse, the Abbé André Morellet, to whom he had written at length on the prospects for peaceable relations between France and Britain. Paine had suggested that there was no interest in war in either court, but that France had an enemy in the vulgar prejudices of the British. He accordingly planned a pamphlet to rectify the misunderstanding between the two peoples. Assured by Morellet of French support, Paine brought out his *Prospects on the Rubicon*, in which the British are offered a stark sense of their choice between war and its many costs, and peace and its benefits. The pamphlet is striking for its support of the French monarchy and its assertion of the common interest between the king and the people.

Paine also canvassed his view that France was committed to peace with leading members of the whig opposition, including Edmund Burke, the marquess of Lansdowne, Charles James Fox, and the duke of Portland, claiming that he was 'in pretty close intimacy with the heads of the opposition' (*Complete Writings*, 2.1276). He hoped for the fall of the Pitt government, believing he would be well placed to act in the capacity of American ambassador to England should the opposition attain power, and he watched closely the unfolding of the regency crisis during the illness of George III in early 1789. Through visits and correspondence he remained well informed about developments in France, and his membership of Lafayette's circle led to him being entrusted with conveying the key of the Bastille to President Washington—a symbol of the common view that America's revolution had provided the spark for change in Europe.

In January 1790 (before Burke's February speech on the army estimates which publicly signalled his abhorrence of the revolution) Paine was engaged in writing an account of the French Revolution. He also corresponded extensively with his English contacts (including Burke), informing them of French affairs. On both counts he drew heavily on letters from Thomas Jefferson. When Burke declared his intention of publishing an attack on the French Revolution Paine committed himself to answering it, and the material he had been preparing was put to this purpose (although there is some indication that he also tried to publish something in French to influence events through Lafayette in the summer of 1790). Burke's *Reflections on the Revolution in France* appeared in November 1790; Paine's response, *Rights of Man*, was printed by Joseph Johnson for publication on 21 February 1791, then withdrawn for fear of prosecution. J. S. Jordan stepped in and published it on 16 March.

Rights of Man opens by taking issue with Burke's understanding of the settlement following the revolution of 1688. Paine counters Burke's insistence that the British people had submitted themselves and their posterity forever to the crown with the claim (broached in his *Dissertations on Government* of 1786) that:

> There never did, there never will, and there never can exist a parliament, or any description of men, or any generation of men, in any country, possessed of the right or the power of binding and controuling posterity to the *end of time*, or of commanding for ever how the world shall be governed, or who shall govern it. . . . Every age and generation must be as free to act for itself, *in all* cases, as the ages and generations which preceded it. (*Complete Writings*, 1.251)

Government is by the living for the living, and each age must be sovereign over its own concerns. Paine then turns to the details of the French case. Continuing to canvass his views from *Prospects*, that the interests of the monarch and his people are united, he insists that the revolution should be understood as one which attacks the despotic principles of the French monarchy, not the king himself. Paine takes the Bastille to symbolize the despotism that had been overthrown, giving a detailed account of the prison's destruction and countering Burke's account of the march on Versailles by the Parisian mob. Returning to his claims about the sufficiency of the rights of each generation, he distinguishes between the natural rights man has by virtue of his existence and his equality before his creator, and the civil rights we create by which we attempt to secure those natural rights that we lack the power perfectly to enjoy. Some natural rights, such as intellectual rights, or rights of the mind, or of religious belief, are rights we have the power to enjoy without needing society's support, but where our power is defective, as in the right to redress, we deposit the natural right in the common stock of society and use society as the means to enforce the right.

Although there are intimations of this view as early as Paine's *Candid and Critical Remarks*...

Ludlow, the fuller development of this position seems to have been worked out one night in France after an evening spent with Jefferson, and possibly Lafayette, discussing a pamphlet by the Philadelphia conservative James Wilson on the proposed federal constitution. On this view, and against Burke, natural rights are the ground and justification for civil rights, they are not simply given up on entering society. Moreover, against Burke's veneration of the English constitution, Paine insists that Britain has no constitution: that its government has arisen out of conquest and has never been generated by a sovereign act of the people. In contrast, the meeting of the estates general provided a convention of the people to form a constitution—which can be compared item by item with its pretended British alternative, as he does. Turning subsequently to give an account of the development of pressure for reform in France leading to the declaration of the rights of man, he suggests that a major role was played by France's involvement in the American War of Independence, through the promulgation of its principles and from the return of those Frenchmen, like Lafayette, who had fought for the Americans. In his final miscellaneous comments he develops an attack on monarchy which reiterates the critique advanced in *Common Sense*, but now emphasizes its significance for the European states of which he had earlier despaired. Quoting Lafayette, he insists that 'For a Nation to be free, it is sufficient that she wills it' (*Complete Writings*, 2.322): 'hereditary governments are verging to their decline, and . . . Revolutions on the broad basis of national sovereignty, and government by representation are making their way in Europe' (ibid., 1.344).

In many respects *Rights of Man* is a disordered mix of narrative, principled argument, and rhetorical appeal—betraying the composite materials Paine used and the speed with which it was composed. But the vigorous and trenchant style in which it was written accounts for its huge success. It was quickly reprinted and widely circulated, with copies being read aloud in inns and coffee houses, so that by May some 50,000 copies were said to be in circulation. Of the 300 or more pamphlets which the revolution controversy spawned, *Rights of Man* was the first seriously to damage Burke's case and to restore credit to the French both in Britain and America.

A republican manifesto

When Paine returned to France in April 1791, those who encountered him found him intoxicated by his success. Étienne Dumont recorded that: 'his egregious conceit and presumptuous self-sufficiency quite disgusted me. He was drunk with vanity. If you believed him, it was he who had done everything in America. He was an absolute caricature of the vainest of Frenchmen' (Keane, 311). Nor was his conviction in the pace of progress dimmed when he was nearly lynched by a Parisian mob for failing to wear a cockade. Indeed, recognizing the increasingly republican spirit animating the French and parting company with Lafayette's circle, especially after the royal family's flight to Varennes, he joined Brissot, Etiènne Chauvière, François du Châtelet, and Condorcet, and, with the help of Nicholas de Bonneville and François Lathenas, established a newspaper, *Le Républicain, ou le défenseur du gouvernement représentatif.* Paine produced a republican manifesto which was translated by Châtelet, printed by Bonneville, and stuck up in the streets of Paris on 1 July. Paine's sense of the common interest between the king and the people had vanished; instead, the flight to Varennes was seen as tantamount to abdication, and he insisted throughout on referring to the king as Louis Capet. Although few supported the declaration, and the Abbé Sieyès engaged Paine in debate in the *Gazette Nationale* on the virtues of elective monarchies, Paine rightly sensed that the tide was turning fast in a republican direction. Following a 4 July dinner in Paris, where Gouverneur Morris thought Paine 'inflated to the Eyes and big with a Litter of revolutions' (*Diary of the French Revolution*, 2.212–13), he returned to England to follow events there and in Ireland more closely, and to work on a book, *Kingship*, which he later changed to a second part of *Rights of Man.*

In England, Paine lived a relatively retired life. He stayed with Thomas 'Clio' Rickman, an old acquaintance from Lewes, and now a London bookseller, and visited John Horne Tooke, who held open house for radicals at his Wimbledon home. In August 1791 he attended a meeting chaired by Tooke at the Thatched House tavern, where a manifesto written by him for Tooke, celebrating events in France and calling for reforms in England, was read and warmly received. His circles of acquaintance also spread to literary radicals such as Mary Wollstonecraft, William Godwin, John 'Walking' Stewart, and William Blake. He also searched for a publisher, since neither Jordan nor Johnson was prepared to accept the risk. Through Thomas Christie he found a Thomas Chapman who was willing to proceed but who, late in the day, sought to persuade Paine to sell him the copyright, and when he was unsuccessful claimed to have had cold feet over the content of the work and refused to proceed. Paine inferred government intervention. He was able to persuade Jordan to take up the printing, indemnifying him by writing a disclaimer in which he claimed to be the sole author and publisher of the work. With a minimum of delay, *Rights of Man: Part the Second,*

Combining Principle and Practice was published on 16 February 1792.

The controversy over the French Revolution is still signalled in Paine's dedication to Lafayette and in some perfunctory comments on Burke and his *Appeal from the New to the Old Whigs* (1791) in the preface. But the introduction switched the focus dramatically by arguing that it is the American War of Independence that has inaugurated the changes that are bringing down the whole order of European despotism. In the first four chapters of the pamphlet it is America, rather than France, which is offered as exemplifying a society united by interest and ruled by a properly constituted representative government. Where in *Common Sense* government was the badge of lost innocence, Paine now treats society as so united by instinct and reciprocal benefits that it needs very little from government. 'The more perfect civilisation is, the less occasion has it for government, because the more does it regulate its own affairs, and govern itself' (*Complete Writings*, 1.358–9).

Paine's attack on monarchy and aristocracy, his insistence that constitutions must arise from conventions of the people and cannot be amended by the governments which they order, and his defence of representative government as taking 'society and civilisation for its basis; nature, reason and experience, for its guide' (ibid., 1.367) are all familiar themes from his earlier writings. But here they are brought together with an unequalled consistency of argument and clarity of presentation and are couched in a thoroughly trenchant, almost insouciant, language. Throughout, the American experience provides a touchstone for the practicality of republican government and the ease with which it can be established. The most innovatory arguments appear in the final chapter (which betray the influence of Paine's contacts with members of the *Comité de Mendicité de la Constituante*, notably Condorcet) when he turns to a detailed examination of the obstacles to commerce and progress in Britain, and in particular to the amount of taxation being raised. Assuming the abolition of the court and its extravagances and the pooling of military expenditure with France and America, Paine argues that government spending could be reduced from £7.5 million to £1.5 million. Rather than cutting tax rates, he proposes a reform of the taxation system together with a whole range of welfare measures. A national system of poor relief financed by taxation would replace local poor rates. Benefits would include child benefit, conditional on attendance at school; supplementary benefits for those over fifty, with a full pension at sixty; a system of maternity and death grants; education for all those in need; a fund for the accommodation and employment of the casual poor of London; and compensation for disbanded soldiers and sailors and their families. Moreover, direct taxation would be replaced by progressive taxation, to be directed against inherited wealth rather than wealth from labour.

Prosecutions in Britain

Writing to John Hall in November 1791 Paine indicated that he was to bring out a new work which he hoped would:

> produce something one way or another. I see the tide is yet the wrong way, but there is a change of sentiment beginning. I have so far got the ear of John Bull that he will read what I write—which is more than ever was done before to the same extent. (*Complete Writings*, 2.1321–2)

Paine's confidence was undiminished when he met Gouverneur Morris shortly after publication of part two of *Rights of Man*, when Morris was on his way to Paris to take up his new post as American ambassador—an appointment Paine regarded as '*a most unfortunate one*' (ibid., 2.1323). Morris recorded: 'He seems Cock Sure of bringing about a Revolution in Great Britain, and I think it quite as likely that he will be promoted to the Pilory' (*Diary of the French Revolution*, 2.368). Over the next six months, while parliamentary whigs sought to distance themselves from Paine's radicalism, the extra-parliamentary movement seized on the pamphlet as a means for mobilizing popular feeling for reform. Cheap editions combining the two parts of *Rights of Man* were published throughout the country, and societies established among members of the artisan classes, such as Thomas Hardy's London Corresponding Society, provided new means for circulating and discussing Paine's work. At the same time, government newspapers attempted to stir up feeling against Paine, and friends persuaded him to decamp to Bromley, where he stayed incognito with William Sharp, the engraver. A visit to London to attend a meeting of the Society for Constitutional Information resulted in his being arrested for a debt of Peter Whiteside an associate in his bridge scheme. He was rescued by Johnson, but the rapid appearance of the story in the press was taken by all as indicating government plotting in the episode. At the end of May 1792, Jordan was indicted for sedition as the publisher of *Rights of Man*. Paine tried to persuade him to fight the case but Jordan chose to plead guilty and pay the fine.

Two weeks later Paine was summoned to answer a charge of seditious libel, and a royal proclamation was issued ordering magistrates to seek out and prosecute those involved in writing or printing wicked and seditious writings. When asked in parliament why the government had delayed so long a prosecution against Paine, the home secretary Henry Dundas (Tooke's next door neighbour) stressed the subversive character of the second part of *Rights of Man* and the determination with which it was being disseminated throughout the kingdom. However Paine refused to be cowed. He wrote an address to the Jacobin Society in Paris claiming that reform societies dedicated to freedom, peace, and the rights of man were springing up throughout the country. In June he published a series of letters, to Dundas and Onslow Cranley, reiterating his scorn for hereditary government and the need for reform, and taunting the government on its decision to postpone his trial until December.

He also produced his *Letter Addressed to the Addressers of the Late Proclamation* (1792), effectively a third part to *Rights of Man*, in which he insisted that representative government relies upon a prior right of manhood suffrage—a principle he had not previously clarified (partly, it seems, to avoid drawing attention to the limits on the franchise within the French constitution). The *Letter* also set out a plan for a British convention to provide for a reform of parliament, a proposal which issued the following year in reform societies taking an increasingly confrontational attitude to the government, and subsequently in draconian sentences being handed down to delegates of the British Convention held in Scotland at the end of 1793 by the lord justice clerk, Lord Braxfield, and in the arrest and indictment for treason of leading English radicals in the summer of 1794. Paine's only concession was to remove the paragraphs upon which his indictment for sedition was based from the six-penny edition published at the beginning of August 1792. Finally, on 13 September, only days after the September massacres in Paris, Paine left London with Achille Audibert and John Frost, took a circuitous route to Dover, where he was detained by a customs officer and searched before eventually being allowed to leave, and, seen off by a hostile crowd, caught the boat for a dramatically changed revolutionary France. He was accorded a contrastingly warm welcome when he landed in Calais.

4 Honorary French citizen

The National Convention and imprisonment

Paine had been one of seventeen foreigners accorded honorary French citizenship in August 1792, and four of the departmental electoral assemblies which met at the beginning of September had elected him as deputy to the new National Convention. Achille Audibert had been in London to urge Paine to accept the seat for Calais and play a part in the new order. He now conducted Paine through the obligatory ceremonies in Calais before seeing him off to attend the opening session of the convention on 21 September. It must quickly have been clear to Paine that he was out of his depth. He spoke little or no French and had to rely on a fellow deputy translating for him, and he had not grasped how dramatically the course of the revolution had changed with the elimination of the monarchy, the eruption of the sans-culottes onto the political scene, and the growing prominence of the Jacobin Club. Only days after the convention opened he sought to challenge Danton's proposal for a purge of the judiciary, only to be swept aside by the convention.

Moreover, while he tried his hand at stirring addresses to the French people, it cannot be said that he showed the political nous which he had demonstrated in America or England. Above all he failed to see that the orderly constitutional process which he had believed to be central to revolution was being swept aside by forces that could no longer be controlled. Some of the forms of order remained: the convention elected him to sit on one of these, a committee of nine (including Sieyès, Condorcet, Brissot, Petion, Barère, and Danton) to design a republican constitution. But, although Paine did not recognize it, it was mainly a form. The committee was dominated by the Brissotins, and its recommendations would stand or fall according to their ability to dominate the more radical Montagnards: they failed, and of the nine members of the committee, only three survived the subsequent eighteen months. However, French success against the Prussians augured well, and the victory at Jemappes led the Brissotins to internationalize the revolution and offer aid to all oppressed people in November, and gave some grounds for Paine's continuing optimism. Sharing the Brissotin mood, Paine now saw no alternative to a revolution in England, and he said as much in an open letter to Archibald MacDonald, the prosecutor in his trial *in absentia* in December 1792, at which he was outlawed.

The Brissotins had resisted bringing the king to trial, but the discovery of incriminating documents in his former apartments in the Tuileries made this position untenable. Paine acknowledged this in his moderate discussion of the issues in *On the Propriety of Bringing Louis XVI to Trial*, but he also sought to save the king's life. After a bare majority had voted for death, Paine sought a reprieve by pressing for detention, and subsequent banishment to America, rather than execution (with Bancal reading a translation of his speech). Marat shouted him down on the grounds that he was a Quaker, and further interruptions by Marat and Thuriot challenged the accuracy of the translation being read and wrecked any chance of his plea finding support.

The king's execution opened the French Revolutionary War, and the Brissotins' power began to crumble. The draft constitution, whose 368 articles and 85 pages ran against Paine's preference for simple structures, was shelved, and Paine's increasing distance from affairs was physically signalled by his move to a house in St Denis, a remote and quiet section of Paris, from which he watched the revolution begin to consume its own leadership. He sought to help the Brissotins when Marat was impeached by reporting a comment Marat made to him when they had first met belittling Paine's belief in republican government. However, the initiative failed and then became dangerously compromising when a fellow boarder, William Johnson, attempted suicide, leaving a note accusing Marat of seeking to extinguish the very liberty he had come to France to enjoy. Although Brissot reported Johnson's dying words, Johnson erred by surviving, and Marat turned the trial into a powerful endorsement. Paine was also involved in the trial of General Miranda, whom he had known in America and who was charged with failing to rally troops at the battle of Neerwinden—on this occasion the charge was being prosecuted by the Jacobins in the hope of discrediting the Brissotins who championed Miranda. Paine was involved solely as a character witness, Miranda was acquitted, but Paine had again come to the attention of the increasingly powerful Jacobins.

On approaching the National Convention on 31 May 1793 Paine was advised by Hanriott, the captain of the guard, to use his deputy's card for hair curlers, and Danton warned him not to go in. Three days later the convention voted to suspend and imprison twenty-two Brissotin members, but these did not include Paine. A few days later a deputation from Arras congratulated the convention on its decision, denounced Paine for his association with the Brissotins, and announced that he no longer represented the interests of the department of Calais. Although he seldom attended the convention, Paine remained willing to try to use his influence where he could, supporting on one occasion a number of American seamen detained in Bordeaux. Indeed, in the summer of 1793 Barère consulted him on the advisability of sending commissioners to America to seek an alliance in the war with Britain. Paine supported the proposal, warning Barère against trusting Gouverneur Morris, who was neither favourable to the French nor well liked in America. A memorandum from Barère's office proposed Paine as one of the commissioners to be sent to America, and Paine worked hard to bring the two nations closer, with Barère crediting him with responsibility for shipments of rice and grain which came from America in 1794. But the proposal came to nothing, and much as Paine wished to return to America (despite news in April that his New

Rochelle house had burnt down) he took no active steps to do so. Within three months Barère had denounced Paine in the National Convention.

On 27 December 1793 the committee of public safety ordered Paine's arrest; a memorandum among Robespierre's papers noted that it was 'for the interests of America as well as of France' (Aldridge, *Man of Reason*, 205), which has encouraged some commentators to think that both Morris and Robespierre wanted Paine out of the way. He was arrested at the Hotel Philadelphia and was required to deliver up his papers. This took all day, and involved Audibert as translator and the poet and diplomatist Joel Barlow as an independent witness, but the soldiers found nothing suspicious. Indeed, they allowed him to hand over to Barlow the manuscript in English of *The Age of Reason* before escorting him to the Luxembourg prison. Three weeks later a group of American citizens led by Barlow petitioned the convention for Paine's release, but found no support. The issue of Paine's citizenship seemed to become pivotal. As a French or British citizen he would be wholly at the mercy of the convention; if American, his government would have a legitimate interest in his case and would have some weight with the French. After representation from Paine, Gouverneur Morris wrote to Deforgues, the minister for foreign affairs, stating that Paine had taken American citizenship during the American War of Independence, although admitting that he had subsequently been accorded French citizenship and had been elected as a member of the National Convention. Deforgues treated Paine's election as overriding any claims he might have had as an American. Conway's biography of Paine was deeply critical of Morris for his inactivity, but without real cause. Morris's conduct, which Conway attributes to his deep dislike of Paine, derived from his view that if Paine kept his head down while in prison, he might contrive to keep it on.

In prison Paine managed to produce (and to convey to Daniel Isaac Eaton, the radical London publisher) a dedication for *The Age of Reason* and a new edition of the *Rights of Man* with a new preface. Other essays written in prison, including one on Robespierre, did not survive, but he successfully maintained a poetic correspondence with an anonymous lady (whom he subsequently learned was the wife of his friend the banker Sir Robert Smyth), who signed herself 'a little corner of the world' to complement his 'the castle in the air'. Conditions in the prison deteriorated during the Terror, and after six months Paine contracted a severe fever which rendered him semi-conscious for several weeks. He was cared for by the prison doctor, Markoshi, and two British inmates, Dr Graham, a physician, and Mr Bond, a surgeon, who successfully brought him through to give him the news of Robespierre's overthrow and execution. Within two weeks Paine was writing to the convention and to the committee of public safety, as were his friends, and when he learned that Morris had been replaced by James Monroe he immediately urged him to take up his case, producing a forty-three page memorial to Monroe insisting on his citizenship. Monroe reassured Paine that he was regarded as an American and entitled to his services, and after he wrote to the convention asking them either to bring Paine to trial or release him the papers were signed for his release. He was delivered from custody on 4 November 1794 and brought to Monroe's house to stay as long as he wished. A month later Antoine-Claire Thibaudeau rose in the convention and successfully proposed that Paine be restored to his seat.

Although Paine played little role in the remaining days of the convention he did adapt a pamphlet written two years earlier in support of his case for eliminating the property qualification for voting from the new constitution. He attended the convention for the first time since his imprisonment in June to have his speech read to his fellow deputies. *Dissertation on the First Principles of Government* (1795) is essentially an epitome of his case in *Rights of Man* and provides an extremely clear and uncluttered statement of his mature views on government. The case for universal manhood suffrage was not, however, obvious to a convention which had been driven by the fury of the Parisian mob over much of the preceding two years, and the new constitution survived Paine's prose to be inaugurated in October 1795. Paine was not elected to it and his official role in France now ended.

The Age of Reason

It is unclear exactly when Paine wrote *The Age of Reason* (Conway, *Life*, 2.100; Hawke, 293, 446). Paine made conflicting statements, but it seems likely that he began early in 1793 and in March was able to turn over a number of completed chapters to Lanthenas for translation and setting. Events in the summer then caused a break in activity, but he returned to the work in the autumn, with Lanthenas translating as he wrote, ensuring that the first edition was published in French, possibly within days of his arrest. In his introduction to part 2 he claimed that he had written the book without either a New or Old Testament to hand, and that he had seen the likelihood of his arrest and had hurriedly drawn the work to a close. Neither circumstance harmed the text. *The Age of Reason* is a trenchant and uncompromising attack on Christianity and all formal religions together with a brief statement of Paine's religious beliefs. More than anything else he wrote it was responsible for the hostility with which he was subsequently treated. Although denounced as epitomizing atheism and infidelity, the work was written with the express design of combating atheism, and it begins with a frank statement of Paine's faith: 'I believe in one God, and no more; and I hope for happiness beyond this life' (*Complete Writings*, 1.464). He disavows both religious institutions, 'All national institutions of churches, whether Jewish, Christian or Turkish, appear to me no other than human inventions, set up to terrify and enslave mankind, and monopolize power and profit' (ibid.), and all revelation, 'A thing which everyone is required to believe requires that the proof and evidence of it should be equal to all, and universal' (ibid., 1.468). The only text which can claim this status is the text of nature: 'THE WORD OF GOD IS THE CREATION WE BEHOLD and it is in *this word*, which no human invention can counterfeit or alter, that God speaketh universally to man' (ibid., 1.482).

Appealing again to the touchstone of common sense, Paine can find nothing to warrant belief in Christianity, and a great many grounds for suspecting imposture.

His arguments follow the pattern of criticism developed in the deist controversy in England in the first quarter of the eighteenth century, but he makes his points in inimitably earthy fashion:

> Whenever we read the obscene stories, the voluptuous debaucheries, the cruel and torturous executions, the unrelenting vindictiveness, with which more than half the bible is filled, it would be more consistent that we called it the word of a demon than the Word of God. (ibid., 1.474)

His deism and the associated account of the order of nature draws heavily on his understanding of celestial mechanics which he learned at the lectures of Benjamin Martin and James Ferguson and provides an alternative vision of the true religion. Soon after his release from prison he began working on part 2 of *The Age of Reason.*

With Old and New Testament now to hand he develops a line of biblical exegesis which shows the conflicting evidence and claims which the Bible contains. Part 2 lacks the power and vision of the first, but it offers instead a careful, often pedantic, critique, book by book, of the Bible's claim to authority—although some books are given lighter treatment, such as Ruth: 'an idle, bungling story, foolishly told, nobody knows by whom, about a strolling country-girl, creeping slyly to bed with her cousin Boaz. Pretty stuff indeed, to be called the Word of God!' (ibid., 1.535). Paine's case is that the Bible must rest its claim to validity on the testimony it contains, but this testimony must itself be unimpeachable, especially given the improbability of the claims made, and that authority evaporates when the testimony is founded to be anonymous and contradictory.

Paine completed part 2 of *The Age of Reason* in August 1795 and left the Monroes for a brief holiday. Within a week he was back with a recurrence of the fever he had in prison and an abscess in his side. He remained seriously ill and bed-ridden, and recovered fully only by the beginning of 1796. During his illness, his long-standing sense of grievance towards America for having forsaken him in the Luxembourg prison finally spilt over, crystallizing into certainty that George Washington had served him treacherously. He wrote a long, acerbic letter to James Madison complaining of Washington's treatment of him. Monroe sought to dissuade Paine, or at least to persuade him that he should not attack the president when he was a guest of his ambassador, but Paine sent at least one angry letter that reached Washington. Moreover, Washington's appointment of John Jay as minister to Britain resulted in a treaty which, to Paine, sacrificed American and French interests to Britain. Paine, and Monroe, feared that the treaty would provoke a breakdown in good relations with France and realign America with her former rulers.

As he recovered from his illness Paine wrote *Agrarian Justice* (1796), the most egalitarian of his works, in which he identified a tendency for civilization to make one part of society more affluent, and the other more wretched, than would have been the case in a natural state. Developing a justification for the redistribution of property that had been absent from *Rights of Man* (and responding in part to the radical challenge to the Directory from Babeuf's Conspiracy of Equals), the pamphlet argues that owners of property owe a ground rent for what they have acquired to the rest of mankind, and that the aim should be to ensure that increased wealth has, and is seen to have, reciprocal benefits for the general mass of society. To achieve this Paine advocated the creation of a national fund, out of which every person arriving at the age of twenty-one would be paid £15 in compensation for the loss of his or her natural inheritance by the introduction of the system of landed property. In addition, each person over the age of fifty would be paid £10 per annum. In both cases this would be a matter of justice, not charity. The English agrarian radical Thomas Spence criticized Paine for not advocating common ownership, but Paine was advancing a doctrine which he believed would be compatible with individual freedom and commercial activity, and which he saw as a necessary bedrock for the political equality that was required to ensure stability within modern states.

Residence in Paris

Within two months of *Agrarian Justice* Paine published *Decline and Fall of the English System of Finance* (1796), an analysis of the financing of the British national debt and its exponential growth which predicted the collapse of the fiscal system as the government sought to fund the current war. The Council of Five Hundred voted for it to be officially printed and distributed, and it served to reintroduce Paine into the political circles of the Directory, which increasingly turned to him for advice on France's relations with America. This, in turn, raised further problems for Monroe, who suspected that Paine was indiscreet with information he obtained by residing with him. Moreover, Paine's anger at Washington resurfaced in public outbursts, and Monroe was finally forced to ask him to find alternative lodgings. Once he had done so—in the spring of 1796 he moved to rooms in Suresnes, a suburb of Paris—there was little to stop him from venting his anger in print. His *Letter to Washington* (1796) is a long, rambling piece, prefaced by an attack on John Jay's treaty and side-swiping at many of America's elder statesmen. The portrait of Washington is unmitigatedly critical, and extends back to accusations of a lacklustre performance as leader of the army during the war. Paine arranged to have it published in America, where it tarnished his reputation still further with the federalists and embarrassed most republicans. It is probably Paine's least likeable publication, even if many found *The Age of Reason* more deeply offensive.

Relations between France and America deteriorated further when Monroe was recalled in November—a decision Paine saw as typical of 'the ingratitude and clandestine manoeuvring of the Government of Washington' (*Complete Writings*, 2.614). Paine, now deeply despondent, decided to return with Monroe, until Monroe pointed out that this might not help him, and so instead he left for Havre-de-Grâce in March 1797 to find a ship. However, his fears for his safety, with English warships stopping and searching American shipping, led to successive delays until, three months later, he gave up and returned to Paris. Nicholas de Bonneville invited him to stay for a week; he was still in residence five years later. Paine's reluctance to risk the journey, and the lack of any corroborating evidence, suggests that the Hambledon Cricket Club's minute for August 1796, which reports Paine's attendance at a club dinner in July 1796, is false!

Paine returned to Paris as the newly elected Council of Five Hundred moved in an increasingly anti-republican direction and sought to reinstate some of the privileges of the Catholic church. In June, Paine criticized proposals to allow the ringing of church bells on the grounds that a stable republican polity required, in addition to equal political rights and a basic level of social and economic equality, a public culture free from the superstitions of Christianity and the power of its religious institutions. Some members of the

Directory clearly shared this view. In January 1797 Paine, the Director La Révellière-Lépaux, and an assorted group of intellectuals and leftists had organized the first meeting of the Théophilanthropy sect, which espoused a broadly rationalist deism, held services revolving around edifying readings, sentimental music, and meditation, and was thought to have the potential to become a state religion.

Paine's sympathies with the Directory were also in evidence in September 1797 when the *coup d'état* of Fructidor purged the council, accorded emergency powers to the Directory, and halted the counter-revolutionary moves. His *Letter of Thomas Paine to the people of France, and the French armies, on the event of the 18th Fructidor, and its consequences* accepts that the revolution had faced a crisis, owing to the 'darksome manoeuvres of a faction' (*Complete Writings*, 2.605), and that the Directory had acted swiftly and without bloodshed to restore public tranquillity. None the less, he insisted that the 1795 constitution remained the best yet devised by human wisdom, and he regretted the necessity of overturning the results of the republic's first free elections. (When, in May 1798, the Directory acted again, in the *coup* of 22 Floreal, against the newly elected left-republicans, Paine said nothing.) Also in his assumed role of adviser, encouraged by Irish republican exiles in Paris, he wrote to the Directory encouraging it to send troops to assist an Irish rebellion. The resulting rising and invasion attempt in August 1798 was a disaster, and the consequent repression destroyed Irish radicalism for a generation.

Paine was also sought out by Bonaparte, who claimed he slept with a copy of *Rights of Man* under his pillow, with whom he discussed the prospects for an invasion of England. In December 1797 he wrote two essays canvassing the design and financing of a fleet of 1000 gunboats to carry an invasion force across the channel, but Bonaparte abandoned the idea of attacking England in favour of Egypt in the first part of 1798. Paine's sense of the increasing betrayal of France by the American administration, now under his long-standing enemy John Adams, may have driven him to the ultimate form of sedition—an article appeared in Bonneville's newspaper *Le Bien Informé* in September 1798 advising the government on the best means to conquer America.

Paine now became increasingly absorbed in non-political matters. He formed a close friendship with the inventor Robert Fulton, revived his interests in matters scientific, and spent much of his time at Bonneville's residence working on bridge models which he cast himself. He visited Dieppe and went on to Bruges to spend several months with Joseph Vanhuele, a fellow inmate of the Luxembourg prison. His finances were in a disastrous state and his bills in Dieppe seem to have been paid by Captain Nathan Haley from Connecticut, a casual friend. The overthrow of the Directory by Bonaparte and the establishment of the Consulate in November 1799 slipped by without comment from Paine. When he returned to Paris and tried to involve himself in the newly arrived commission from America, he was warned by the Foreign Office that they considered his behaviour irregular and that he would be sent back to America at the first complaint against him.

Paine revived thoughts of returning to America when he heard that Thomas Jefferson was likely to be elected president as Adams's successor, and he wrote a spate of letters to Jefferson in October 1800, including an essay entitled *Compact Maritime* on the desirability of an international association of nations dedicated to protect the rights of commerce. These went unanswered until March, when Jefferson's reply offered him a place on a public ship due to return soon and informed him that an old friend of Paine's, Robert Livingston, would be the next minister to France. Paine deferred acceptance, saying he would await Livingston's arrival, imagining that if he delayed he might be offered a public post. To Jefferson's embarrassment, he published a copy of the letter. The peace of Amiens, signed in March 1802, gave him the opportunity to return safely. Six months later, having arranged for Bonneville's family to follow him, and with his financial

80 problems largely solved by a gift of about £500 (from Francis Burdett and William Bosville), he set off again for Havre-de-Grâce, accompanied by Thomas 'Clio' Rickman, who came to bid him farewell.

5

Death of a democrat

Return to America

Paine arrived in Baltimore on 18 October 1802 to a seemingly friendly reception. But the impression was fleeting. He was temporarily arrested on a dubious charge of indebtedness, and the federalists immediately sought to make capital of Paine's irreligion and Thomas Jefferson's offer of a public vessel. When he arrived in Washington only Jefferson and the most ardent republicans welcomed him. Even old colleagues, such as Benjamin Rush and Samuel Adams, turned against him because of his religious heterodoxy. And when he wielded his pen against the federalists in a series of seven letters, *To the Citizens of the United States*, written between November 1802 and April 1803, he often provided his enemies with ammunition against himself and his friends. He supported Jefferson both publicly and privately over the Louisiana purchase in 1803, and gave copious advice to James Monroe, who was sent as minister extraordinary to negotiate over the purchase with the French government. When he suspected Jefferson of a certain coolness toward him and wrote in protest, the president's reply was warm and gracious, and satisfied Paine of his continuing affection. He left Washington in February and visited Bordentown. When he tried to catch the coach on to New York he was refused admittance by the coachman on account of his infidelity, and a crowd hissed and booed him as he left on horseback.

Paine's reception in New York was friendlier, with a testimonial dinner being held in his honour. He spent much of the next few months visiting friends and arranging for a cottage on his New Rochelle estate to be enlarged, although he also talked of returning to France should Napoleon's campaign against England be successful (and in 1804 wrote an epistle *To the People of England on the Invasion of England* to assist that end). Although received warmly by friends and fellow republicans his proposal to publish a third part of *The Age of Reason* was the cause of trepidation, and Nicolli Fosdick wrote to Jefferson, warning him that Paine was in the habit of reading out aloud letters from Jefferson which were best kept confidential, and encouraging the president to dissuade Paine from further publications on religious matters.

In the summer of 1804 Paine settled again in New Rochelle. He arranged for Marguerite de Bonneville, the wife of a Parisian friend who had arrived in the summer of 1803, and whom he had lodged in his house at Bordentown, to move to New York and secured her employment as a French teacher, but financial difficulties quickly developed. They agreed that he should take her three sons into his care and see to their education at New Rochelle, but their mother seemed both to want them with her without being willing either to live at New Rochelle (because it was too quiet) or to have the children with her in

New York. Her husband remained in France. On Christmas eve, 1805, Christopher Derrick, whom Paine had employed to look after the farm while in New York the previous year, combined an overindulgence in drink with bottled-up resentment against Paine and fired a musket at him while he was reading in his living room. Paine escaped without harm. Characteristically, he refused to press charges.

Paine continued to write—an eighth and final letter *To the Citizens of the United States* in June 1805, against the federalists; *Constitutions, Governments, and Charters* (also in June), in which he argued that the legislature proposing charters should not have the power to make them law; a brief *Remarks on English Affairs* in July 1805, which contained such positive comments on Napoleon that Thomas Rickman, who had heard Paine's private views, declined to believe Paine was the author; and the essays *The Origin of Freemasonry* and *Constitutional Reform.* The following year he produced the speculative *The Cause of Yellow Fever* and returned briefly to the federalists and affairs in Europe, and in 1807 wrote several essays on the use of gun boats and on the likelihood of war with Britain. But his health and powers were gradually fading, and he kept sliding into financial difficulties, from which he extracted himself by selling, reluctantly, parts of his farm. He tried to interest Jefferson and George Clinton in asking congress to take up the issue of financial acknowledgement for his services to the War of Independence, but although efforts were made nothing came of them, and Jefferson turned down Paine's offer to act as a special envoy to Napoleon.

In the spring of 1806 Paine left the farm to lodge in a local inn, where his friend William Carver found him weeks later, dishevelled, unshaven, drunk, and a good deal the worse for wear. Carver brought him to live with him in New York, but in June Paine had a fit of apoplexy and was so badly injured he was bed-ridden for weeks, nursed by Mrs Palmer, the widow of Paine's deist friend Elihu. On doctor's advice he moved from Carver's to lodge with John Wesley Jarvis, a portrait painter, in November. Carver then sent him a bill for his lodgings, and for the services of Mrs Palmer. His health improved and Jarvis reported him 'one of the pleasantest companions I have met with for an old man' (Aldridge, *Man of Reason*, 296). In November 1806 he visited New Rochelle to vote in the congressional elections, but the election inspector, Elisha Ward, refused to register his vote, insisting that he was not an American citizen—a charge Paine sought to challenge in the courts. When Jarvis moved in April 1807, Paine found lodgings with Zakarias Hitt—a disciple of Paine's—who lived on the outskirts of New York. When Hitt raised his rent the following January Paine insisted he could not afford to pay, despite his continued ownership of property at both New Rochelle and Bordentown. He also insisted on writing to congress to ask for the reimbursement of his expenses for the trip he had taken to France with Laurens twenty-five years earlier. Congress demurred and an offer on the farm fell through, and he moved to a cheap tavern in February, where he remained until removed by friends in July. The Bordentown farm was sold for $800 and a new lodging was found in Greenwich Village.

Paine had now lost the use of his legs and he grew increasingly weaker. By January 1809 he needed constant care and he set out his will, in which the bulk of the estate went to Madame Bonneville for the education of her children. He asked the Quakers to allow him to be buried in their burial-ground, but was refused, and he made Madame Bonneville promise that he would be buried on his New Rochelle farm. In May, overwhelmed by his isolation, he persuaded Madame Bonneville to rent a house in which to care for him. He moved in with her on 4 May to 59 Grove Street in Greenwich Village and died at 8 o'clock in the morning of 8 June 1809. He was buried at New Rochelle, mourned by his black servant, Madame Bonneville, her son Benjamin, and a handful of local people. In 1819 the former tory turned radical William Cobbett had his bones dug up and brought back to England, where they subsequently disappeared.

Personality, principles, and reputation

The first biography of Paine was published in the summer of 1791, with government encouragement, by George Chalmers (under the pseudonym Francis Oldys), a government clerk in the Board of Trade and an accomplished and serious writer. The work is the sole source for a great many of the stories about Paine's life prior to his departure for America, but its thirst for information is coupled with an evident antipathy to its subject. However, it is only in the second edition of 1793 that any reference is made to Paine's drinking. Thereafter, accusations of drunkenness and associated slovenly habits become commonplace in reports of Paine. These reached new heights in the biography produced by James Cheetham, published shortly after Paine's death. Cheetham, a former radical and newspaper editor, had fallen out with Paine in 1806 and presented him as a hopeless drunkard and atheist, portraying the symptoms and side effects of Paine's stroke and deteriorating health as evidence of his alcoholism. Subsequent favourable biographies of Paine, notably Rickman's in 1819 and the first scholarly biography by M. D. Conway in 1892, tend to the opposite extreme, and tend also to underplay Paine's increasing egoism and vanity.

From a wide variety of sources it seems clear that Paine drank to excess, especially when under strain; that he could be extremely lazy and self-indulgent; that he was prone to exaggerate his contribution to the world of politics, theology, and philosophy; that he lacked restraint in expounding his principles in company; that he bragged of disinterestedness in publishing as he did, then clamoured for compensation; that he was a hopeless manager of money and was not particular about repaying his debts; that in matters of dress and appearance he fell short of the standards of many of his contemporaries; and that his once rather handsome appearance was ravaged by his indulgence in alcohol. Moreover, after his imprisonment and illness these faults were exacerbated and his bitterness over his fate frequently clouded his judgement.

But, alongside these faults, which contemporaries assiduously recorded and relayed, and which most biographers have subsequently either ignored or magnified, there are many other reports, often from unlikely quarters, of an entertaining conversationalist, with considerable charm and an engaging manner—even if he was capable of reciting the most part of his major works by heart, while insisting that there was nothing to be gained by going back to earlier writers. If there is a balanced picture to be had, it is that he was a man from a poor background in an aristocratic age, whose capacity to offend was increasingly enhanced by his lack of deference and his sense of his own importance. That sense may have irritated his contemporaries, but it was not misplaced: he was an extremely effective pamphleteer, with a capacity to capture and relay ideas and principles of which his audience had hitherto only an inchoate appreciation.

Paine's originality is frequently disparaged, but he offers a powerful and distinctive account of the principles of democratic politics in which political and civil equality are supported by a degree of social and economic equality. Although commentators often stress the similarities of his account to John Locke's *Second Treatise of Civil Government*, despite Paine's claim never to have read it, there is nothing in Locke to match Paine's redistributive policies, his sense of his intimate connection between equal citizenship and political stability, or his insistence on the universalism of his political ideas and citizenship. And although his religious writings did most to stir up hostility against him for 100 years or more—with Teddy Roosevelt describing him in 1888 as 'a filthy little atheist' (Roosevelt, 289)—many working-class readers found in them the resources with which to rethink their religious commitments, just as the other writings allowed them to rework their politics.

Although his precise intellectual and historical importance remains disputed, Paine is now accepted as a leading figure in the age of revolutions. Collections of his work have appeared regularly since his death, with M. D. Conway making the most important contribution at the end of the nineteenth century with a four-volume collection. A two-volume collection, edited by Philip Foner in 1945, remains the most comprehensive, but is far from complete and is flawed in some parts. No comprehensive bibliography has yet appeared. Statues of him have been erected in Paris, in the Parc Montsouris, and in Thetford, and one is mooted for Washington; active Tom Paine societies exist in both Britain and America, with regular meetings and newsletters, and the United States postal service issued a commemorative stamp with Paine's head in January 1968. He has also been the subject of a novel by Howard Fast, *Citizen Tom Paine* (1945), and several plays, notably Paul Foster's *Tom Paine* (1967) and Jack Shepherd's *In Lambeth* (1990).

Sources

The complete writings of Thomas Paine, ed. P. S. Foner, 2 vols. (Secaucus, New Jersey, 1945) · F. Oldys [G. Chalmers], *The life of Thomas Paine* (1791/3) · J. Cheetham, *The life of Thomas Paine* (1809) · C. Rickman, *Life of Thomas Paine* (1819) · M. D. Conway, *The life of Thomas Paine, with a history of his literary, political, and religious career in America, France, and England*, 2 vols. (1892) · M. D. Conway, *Thomas Paine (1737–1809) et la révolution dans les deux mondes* (Paris, 1900) · A. O. Aldridge, *Man of reason: the life of Thomas Paine* (1960) · A. O. Aldridge, *Thomas Paine's American ideology* (Cranbury, New Jersey, 1984) · D. F. Hawke, *Paine* (1974) · *A diary of the French Revolution by Gouverneur Morris*, ed. B. C. Davenport, 2 vols. (1939) · H. R. Yorke, *Letters from France in 1802*, 2 vols. (1804) · J. Keane, *Tom Paine: a political life* (1995) · J. Fruchtman, *Thomas Paine: apostle of freedom* (New York, 1994) · J. Fruchtman, *Thomas Paine and the religion of nature* (Baltimore, 1993) · G. Claeys, *Thomas Paine: social and political thought* (1989) · E. Foner, *Tom Paine and revolutionary America* (New York, 1976) · E. Foner, *Tom Paine: collected writings* (1995) · D. A. Wilson, *Paine and Cobbett: the transatlantic connection* (Montreal, 1988) · B. Bailyn, *Faces of revolution: personalities and themes in the struggle for American independence* (New York, 1990) · R. R. Fennesey, *Burke, Paine, and the 'Rights of Man'* (The Hague, 1963) · R. Gimbel, *Thomas Paine: a bibliographical checklist of 'Common sense'* (New Haven, 1956) · W. H. G. Armytage, 'Thomas Paine and the Walkers: an early episode in Anglo-American cooperation',

Pennsylvania History, 18 (1951), 16–30 · H. H. Clark, 'An historical interpretation of Thomas Paine's religion', *University of California Chronicle*, 35 (1933), 56–87 · H. H. Clark, 'Introduction', *Thomas Paine: representative selections, with introduction, bibliography and notes* (1944) · J. G. James, 'Thomas Paine's iron bridge work, 1785–1803', *Newcomen Society Transactions*, 57 (1987–8), 189–221 · 'Paine and science', *Enlightenment and dissent*, 16 (1998) · D. Abel, 'The significance of the letter to the Abbé Raynal in the progress of Thomas Paine's thought', *Pennsylvania Magazine of History and Biography*, 66 (1942), 176–90 · I. Kramnick, 'Tom Paine: radical liberal', *Republicanism and bourgeois radicalism: political ideology in late-eighteenth century England and America* (Ithaca, 1990) · I. Dyck, ed., *Citizen of the world: essays on Thomas Paine* (New York, 1988) · I. Dyck, 'Local attachments, national identities and world citizenship in the thought of Thomas Paine', *History Workshop Journal*, 35 (1993), 117–35 · G. Kates, 'From liberalism to radicalism: Tom Paine's *Rights of Man*', *Journal of the History of Ideas*, 50 (1989), 569–87 · *The autobiography of Benjamin Rush*, ed. G. W. Corner (1948) · C. Robbins, 'The lifelong education of Thomas Paine (1737–1809): some reflections on his acquaintance among books', *Proceedings of the American Philosophical Society*, 127 (1983), 135–42 · J. Turner, 'Burke, Paine, and the nature of language', *Yearbook of English studies: the French Revolution in English literature and art*, ed. J. R. Watson, special number, 19 (1989), 75–92 · E. A. Payne, 'Tom Paine: preacher', *Times Literary Supplement* (31 May 1947), 267 · T. Roosevelt, *Gouverneur Morris* (Boston, 1888) · T. Copeland, 'Burke, Paine, and Jefferson', *Edmund Burke: six essays* (1950), 146–89 · F. K. Prochaska, 'Thomas Paine's "The age of reason revisited" ', *Journal of the History of Ideas*, 33 (1972), 561–76 · A. Williamson, *Thomas Paine: his life, work and times* (1973) · A. J. Ayer, *Thomas Paine* (1988) · W. E. Woodward, *Tom Paine: America's godfather, 1737–1809* (1945) · A. Thomson, 'Thomas Paine and the United Irishmen', *Études Irlandaises*, 16 (1991), 109–19 · B. Vincent, *Thomas Paine, ou la religion de la liberté* (Paris, 1987) · B. Vincent, ed., *Thomas Paine, ou la république sans frontières* (Nancy, 1993)

Index